Orcas

By Dionna L. Mann

Bookmobile
Fountaindale Public Library
Bolingbrook, IL
(630) 759-2102

Children's Press®

An Imprint of Scholastic Inc.

Content Consultants
Becky Ellsworth
Curator, Shores
Columbus Zoo and Aquarium

Library of Congress Cataloging-in-Publication Data
Names: Mann, Dionna L., author.
Title: Orcas/by Dionna Mann.
Description: New York, NY: Children's Press, an imprint of Scholastic Inc., [2019] | Series: Nature's children | Includes index.
Identifiers: LCCN 2018023396| ISBN 9780531127186 (library binding) | ISBN 9780531134306 (paperback)
Subjects: LCSH: Killer whale—Juvenile literature.
Classification: LCC QL737.C432 M36 2019 | DDC 599.53/6—dc23

Design by Anna Tunick Tabachnik

Creative Direction: Judith E. Christ for Scholastic Inc.

Produced by Spooky Cheetah Press

Printed in Heshan, China   62

SCHOLASTIC, CHILDREN'S PRESS, NATURE'S CHILDREN™, and associated logos
are trademarks and/or registered trademarks of Scholastic Inc.

1 2 3 4 5 6 7 8 9 10 R 28 27 26 25 24 23 22 21 20 19

Scholastic Inc., 557 Broadway, New York, NY 10012.

Photographs ©: cover: Gerard Lacz/FLPA/Minden Pictures; 1: benymarty/iStockphoto; 4 leaf silo and throughout:
stockgraphicdesigns.com; 4 top: Jim McMahon/Mapman ®; 5 child silo: All-Silhouettes.com; 5 orca silo and throughout:
Yauheniya Piatrouskaya/Dreamstime; 5 bottom: Gerard Lacz/age fotostock; 7: Calvin Hall/Getty Images;
8: Musat/iStockphoto; 11: ARCO/P. Wegner/age fotostock; 12: John Hyde/Design Pics/Getty Images;
15: Ton Wu/NPL/Minden Pictures; 16: jonmccormackphoto/iStockphoto; 19 top right: Yann-HUBERT/iStockphoto;
19 top left: fieldwork/iStockphoto; 19 bottom left: Paul Souders/Getty Images; 19 bottom right: Johnny Adolphson/Shutterstock;
20: Paul Nicklen/Getty Images; 23: Pablo Cersosimo/robertharding/Getty Images; 25: Flip Nicklin/Minden Pictures;
26: Volvox Inc/Alamy Images; 29: Gerard Lacz Images/Superstock, Inc.; 30: Doug Allan/NPL/Minden Pictures;
33: Julie Selan; 34: Flip Nicklin/Minden Pictures; 37: Ragnar Th. Sigurdsson/age fotostock; 38: Fiona Goodall/Getty Images;
41: SeaPics.com; 42 bottom: Jelger Herder/Buiten-beeld/Minden Pictures; 42 center left: Franco Banfi/Getty Images;
42 center right: cmeder/iStockphoto; 42 top: Dave Fleetham/Design Pics/Getty Images; 43 top left: Ochocki Gregory/Getty
Images; 43 top right: chonlasub woravichan/Shutterstock; 43 bottom: chasty/age fotostock.

◀ Cover image shows
an orca leaping from
the water.

Table of Contents

Fact File: Orcas

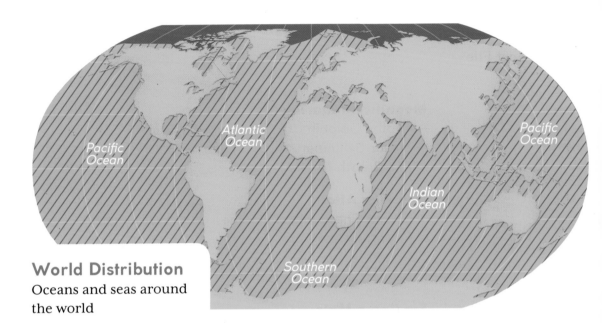

Pacific Ocean

Atlantic Ocean

Pacific Ocean

Indian Ocean

Southern Ocean

World Distribution
Oceans and seas around the world

Habitat
Aquatic marine habitats from the polar regions to the equator

Habits
Live underwater but surface to breathe; travel, hunt, and socialize within close-knit family groups called pods

Diet
Marine mammals, seabirds, fish, squid, octopus, rays, sea turtles

Distinctive Features
Large black-and-white body; tall black triangular dorsal fin; grayish-white saddle patch

Fast Fact
An adult male's dorsal fin can reach 6 ft. (1.8 m) tall.

Average Size

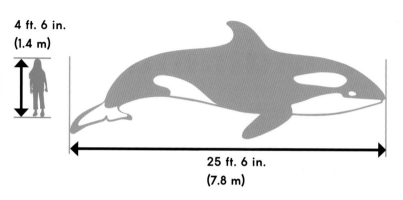

4 ft. 6 in.
(1.4 m)

25 ft. 6 in.
(7.8 m)

Human (age 10)

Orca (adult)

Classification

CLASS
Mammalia
(mammals)

ORDER
Cetacea
(whales)

FAMILY
Delphinidae
(oceanic dolphins)

GENUS
Orcinus
(orca)

SPECIES
Orcinus orca
(killer whale)

◀ Male orca offspring
live their entire lives
with their mothers.

CHAPTER 1

Magnificent Marine Mammals

Look! Over there! What are those tall black triangles moving through the icy-cold water? They're dorsal fins jutting toward the sky. They are moving slowly and silently through the frigid waters off the coast of Washington State. All at once, a huge black-and-white body breaks the surface. It lunges into the air. It spins backward and lands with a tremendous splash. Another body leaps and dives. Then another, and another. It's a group of orcas on the move. We can't hear them, but they are communicating with one another beneath the water. That's why they slip through the water like sleek submarines following a commander. There's nothing quite like them in nature—a family of animals that plays, works, moves, and lives together in perfect harmony.

▶ Orcas are very acrobatic animals. They can jump more than 10 ft. (3 m) out of the water.

Fast Fact

An orca's cone-shaped teeth are up to 4 in. (10.2 cm) long.

Toothy Dolphin

Orcas are the largest member of the dolphin family. Like the other marine mammals in this family, orcas are classed as toothed whales. And they have lots of them— 40 razor-sharp, interlocking teeth. Orcas don't use their teeth for chewing. They use them for grabbing, tearing, and ripping prey. Then they gulp their meal down. If an orca loses a tooth, it won't be replaced by a new one.

Orcas are apex predators, which is why they are called killer whales. They sit at the top of the ocean's food chain. Orcas are not hunted by any other animals. No matter how large, smart, or fast the prey, it's no match for an orca. Despite their scary name and reputation, orcas don't attack humans in the wild. Like all wild animals, orcas kill to eat. They kill to survive.

◀ Growth layers of an orca's teeth can help researchers estimate its age.

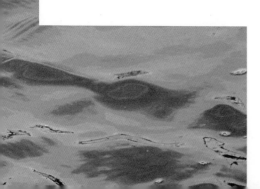

Stellar Swimmer

Orcas are really big. An orca is almost as long and heavy as a school bus! Its body is shaped sort of like a torpedo—cylindrical and tapering at both ends. It's a perfect design for swimming and for water acrobatics. Orcas can leap out of the water to briefly soar above the surface. That's called breaching. Orcas can also spin and do blackflips through the air. They do belly flops and somersaults, too. When orcas want speed, they'll porpoise. That's when they breach, then dive over and over again in a forward motion. At top speed, orcas can reach 30 miles (48.3 kilometers) per hour.

Orcas have amazing maneuverability underwater, too. They twist, turn, flip, and move with grace. How are they able to accomplish such amazing feats? The entire back third of an orca's body is solid muscle, and the flukes on its tail are like engines.

Fast Fact
A male orca is about two times bigger around than a female.

Flukes
enables the orca to accelerate, decelerate, rotate, leap, and stop on a dime.

Saddle Patch

is like a fingerprint— every orca's is different!

Dorsal Fin

keeps the orca steady as it swims.

Blowhole

closes with a watertight seal when the orca is underwater.

Pectoral Flippers

are used for steering.

Melon

is the round fatty part of the orca's forehead that the animal uses to hear.

11

Fast Fact
Orcas can hold their breath underwater for up to 15 minutes.

The Breath of Life

Orcas are mammals that live underwater. They're not like fish, which have gills. Orcas don't get their oxygen from the water. Like humans, they have lungs. Orcas must hold their breath when underwater and rise to the surface every time they have to breathe.

An orca can't breathe through its mouth, and it doesn't have what we would recognize as a nose. Instead, an orca breathes through its blowhole, which is perfectly positioned at the top of the head. Once the orca's blowhole breaks the surface, the animal can take in air.

Orcas are voluntary breathers. In other words, they must consciously decide when to breathe. When orcas realize they need air, they rise toward the water's surface. They contract a muscular flap that covers the blowhole. They exhale. *Phoooo!* Then the orca is ready to take another deep breath in.

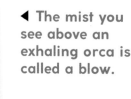

◄ The mist you see above an exhaling orca is called a blow.

13

CHAPTER 2

A Family Affair

Orcas are all about family. They live together in family groups called pods. All the animals in the group are related on the mother's side of the family. An orca pod is **matriarchal**, which means the oldest female is boss. Where she goes, everybody goes. What she hunts, everybody hunts. The female in charge might be the mother, grandmother, or great-grandmother of the other orcas! Sometimes an older female separates to form her own pod with her direct offspring. If she does, the female will stay close by her original pod.

Orca pods share their mother's dialect—a unique set of calls and whistles. This dialect is passed down from generation to generation. Orca pods use these **vocalizations** to communicate with one another. When related pods are separated but traveling nearby, they use their dialect to send out long-distance calls to get together to socialize.

▶ Orca pods range in size from four whales to 50, sometimes more.

Calling These Waters Home

Orcas are at home in any ocean or sea from South Africa to Alaska. The largest **population** hangs out in colder waters. They really like the waters of coastal areas.

Orca pods that spend time in the same waters year-round are called residents. Orca pods that stay for a time in one region and then move on to the next are called transients. Transient orcas might roam from the Antarctic to the tropics, then back again! When traveling, orcas **navigate** using **echolocation**. In an orca community, residents and transients get along fine. They don't fight over the same food source.

Orcas are warm-blooded, but they don't **migrate** during winter to stay warm. They carry the perfect protection against frigid temperatures right within their bodies, called **blubber**. It is a thick layer of fat insulation below their skin that can be up to 4 inches (10.2 centimeters) thick.

◀ Orcas swim in the Salish Sea off the coast of Washington.

Powerful Predators

Orcas are not born knowing how to hunt. Their mothers teach them techniques for taking down very diet-specific prey. It's a family culture, passed down from mother to offspring over generations. Some orcas hunt penguins, porpoises, or sea lions. Others eat stingrays, octopi, or squid. Some pods find walruses or whales delicious. Diet also depends on what's available in the orca's **habitat**.

Orcas are clever predators. They are also masters at hunting as a team. Take the orcas that enjoy the meat of the mighty great white shark. They have learned that if they flip the shark bottom side up, it's unable to move. It takes **stealth** and skillful planning to flip a great white like a pancake without getting chomped. First, the orcas harass the great white until it gets tired. They keep it from deep-diving. They swim under it, around it, and above it. Then, when the shark is exhausted—*wham!* Body slam! The great white is **stunned**, flipped over, and rendered motionless. Shark meat coming up!

▶ To see what orcas are eating, scientists test DNA in living orcas' poop.

Penguin

Some Antarctic orcas are picky, eating t the penguin's breast.

Ray

▶ New Zealand orcas eat stingrays, eagle rays, and electric rays.

Walrus

A 3,300 lb. (1,496.9 kg.) walrus can pply an orca with loads of calories.

Salmon

In the North Pacific, salmon make up 96 percent of a resident orca's diet.

Gone Fishing

The orcas that hunt fish are also very clever. Those living near Norway, for example, have learned a smart way to hunt Atlantic herring. First, they use echolocation to find a school of fish. Then they determine the direction the school is traveling and how fast it's moving. As a team, the orcas race toward the school and begin herding the fish. They encircle the school and make loud bursts of sound. They spin their bodies, flash their white bellies, and blow bubbles. The fish panic. They cluster into a ball. Then the orcas slap the outside of the ball with their flukes, stunning the fish on the outside edge. *Gulp! Gulp!* The orcas take turns feasting. They eat one fat herring after another while the other orcas keep herding the fish.

◀ Each successful slap of an orca's tail can provide 15 herring to eat.

Masters of the Sneak Attack

Orcas use their smarts to hunt marine mammals, too. Antarctic orcas use the wave method to hunt. Once they've spotted a seal lounging on an ice floe, an orca emits an underwater call. Pod members line up. They dive a few feet beneath the water's surface. Then...charge! Their massive bodies and powerful flukes push the water. A rolling wave heads for the unsuspecting seal. The swell tips the ice floe, and the seal slips into the water. Lunch is served.

Then there are the orcas of Argentina. They use the sneak attack when hunting sea lion pups that play on the shore. When the tide is just right, an orca uses echolocation to spy the pup. As a wave rolls in, the orca emerges from the shallows and darts onshore. It purposely beaches itself. The orca seizes the pup in its jaws and turns around. Then the orca waits for the next wave to carry it back to the safety of the water.

▶ Smooth stones on the shoreline enable the orca to slide back out to sea.

CHAPTER 3

Finding a Mate

Marine biologists who study orcas under human care have learned a lot about reproduction. They know that females usually **mate** when they are about 20 years old. Orcas will mate at any time of the year. In the wild, females are more likely to become pregnant when food is plentiful. Males are also more likely to reproduce when they're big and fat.

Orcas don't normally choose to mate with close relatives. Brothers, first cousins, and uncles are not considered suitable mates to a female orca. But how can she find a mate that's not a close relative if all the males traveling with her are closely related? The female pays close attention when her pod is socializing with pods not related to hers. If she hears a male make whistles and calls that are different from her family's dialect, she knows the male is not a relative.

▶ Orcas under human care help us understand behavior in the wild.

Orca Babies

Once orcas mate, the male returns to his pod, and the
pregnant female returns to hers. After a 17- to 18-month
gestation, she's ready to give birth. Orca babies are born
underwater. The newborn's tail usually emerges first.
While the mother swims, she pushes until her baby plops
out. Females give birth to a single calf. Only one instance
of orca twins has ever been documented.

A newborn orca can weigh from 200 to 400 pounds
(90.7 to 181.4 kilograms) and measure 7 to 8 feet (2.1 to
2.4 meters) long! As soon as the orca is born, its mother
helps it surface for its first breath. Then they go back
underwater. The baby is ready to take on life at sea, where
it will swim snug beside its mother.

It will be three to five years before the female becomes
pregnant again. A female orca will have only four to six
offspring in her lifetime.

◀ Female orcas stop
breeding when they're
about 40 years old.

27

Magnificent Milk

Newborn orcas need a lot of fatty calories to build up their blubber. They won't survive without that insulating fat. An orca mother's milk contains 30 to 50 percent fat. That's 10 times as fatty as cow's milk!

How does a calf **nurse** underwater? First, the mom swims near the surface, rolls slightly to her side, and arches her tail. The calf takes a deep breath. It dives beneath its mom's belly. It sticks its mouth inside a slit where the mother's milk is tucked away. Having no lips for suckling, the calf sticks out its tongue to form a seal. Mom responds by shooting milk into her baby's mouth.

Newborn calves nurse for about 5 to 10 seconds at a time, several times an hour, all day and night. Mom stays near the surface so the calf can take breaths between feedings. During its first year of life, the calf can gain 900 lb. (408.2 kg) and grow at least 2 ft. (0.6 m)!

▶ Orca milk is thick, with the consistency of toothpaste.

Taking Care of Junior

Orca calves stop nursing when they're about 2 years old. Then they'll need meat to eat—lots of it. Mothers hunt for their young. Other pod members share their food with junior, too. Sharing food is the orca way.

Juveniles spend years learning how to hunt by watching other members of the pod. They swim close to their mothers until it's time for the attack. Then they hover at a safe distance to watch and learn.

Mothers are often seen tossing stunned but live prey such as seals to their youngsters. Mom is not just playing with her meal. She's allowing her youngster to practice catching the seal and hitting it back into the air with its flukes. The youngster is learning how to stun prey. Practice makes perfect!

Orcas protect their young. They won't allow the youngsters to participate in the hunt or hunt alone until they're ready.

◄ A pod of orcas prepares to knock a sea lion off an ice floe.

CHAPTER 4

Ancient Orcas

In 1882, Spinello Ortolani was doing some planting on a farm near Cetona, Italy. His spade hit some very special stones. Ortolani had discovered fossils. More digging unearthed a partial skull, teeth, ribs, and vertebrae—ancient remains of a close relative of the orca.

Orcinus citoniensis, as the animal is known today, was about 13 ft. (4 m) long and had more teeth than modern-day orcas. Scientists say it lived 3.66 million to 2.58 million years ago, during the Piacenzian age. To date, no older fossil has been found that's closer on the orca's family tree.

When the 19th-century paleontologist Giovanni Capellini studied *Orcinus citoniensis*, he could tell it was an ancient toothed whale. How? He studied the structure of the skull. He could tell with certainty that the animal once used the echolocation system. He knew it was much like a living orca.

▶ Scientists think this is what *Orcinus citoniensis* looked like.

Close Cousins

Orcas are members of the Delphinidae family. This family includes dolphins that live in the ocean, pilot whales, and right whales. There are more than 30 species in this family. The bottlenose dolphin is probably the most recognizable. Some oceanic dolphins have short beaks, others long. Some have dorsal fins; others don't. Some prefer warm climates, others cold. All use echolocation and vocalizations to communicate. All nurse their young and have lungs. All have teeth and are carnivores.

Marine biologists list all orcas as one species, but they also categorize them into ecotypes. That's because some have developed physical and cultural differences that set them apart from others. The adult males of one ecotype are big, up to 31 ft. (9.5 m) long. The adult males of another are small, only about 20 ft. (6.1 m) long. The skin of another ecotype has a brownish hue. These orcas also have stumpy dorsal fins. Yet another ecotype has teeny-tiny eye patches and bulging foreheads.

◄ Like orcas, bottlenose dolphins are intelligent and social animals.

CHAPTER 5

Humans and Orcas

Most people have to visit an aquarium to get up close to an orca. Others climb aboard whale-watching boats. They hope for an eye-to-eye encounter with wild orcas. After seeing orcas in the wild, people often want to protect them and safeguard their natural habitat.

Imagine being in a small boat and discovering that a pod of thirty orcas is headed your way. They encircle your little vessel. A mother and her calf pass right under you. The baby looks right at you! You feel the spray from their blow as they surface to breathe. Then one of them breaches completely out of the water. You feel cold water splash on your skin. Amazing? Incredible? Unbelievable? Does your heart race? That's how people respond when they experience an up-close encounter with an orca pod. Orca encounters are known to be, in a word, awesome.

▶ Respectful whale watchers in big vessels give orcas room to hunt.

Orcas on Alert

Some orca populations are **endangered**. Many things can cause orca babies to die, or make orcas get sick. The orcas' food supply might be low or it might contain chemical pollution. Or the orca may have had to swim through an oil spill.

Scientists like to keep a close eye on endangered orca populations. They try to figure out why the population isn't growing. Why did an individual or a baby die? Why did one of them get stuck on the beach? Researchers take blubber samples from the stranded orca. They examine the dead bodies of orcas that wash up onshore. When an orca pod is sighted, they rush out in their boats to photograph the animals' fins and saddle patches. They determine which pod it is, what individuals are still alive, or who may have had a baby. They record everything and share their findings with other researchers.

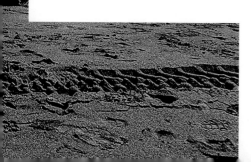

◀ Every year, orcas are severely injured or killed by boat strikes.

A Real-Life Miracle!

On August 23, 1993, New Zealand orcas were hunting in the shallows for stingrays. A young, inexperienced female was among the group. During the hunt, she became stranded on the beach! Her family waited, helpless, just off the beach. All they could do was call to her. She needed human help.

Thankfully, someone saw the young orca thrashing on the sand. Soon, trained volunteers arrived. To keep the orca alive, they hydrated her skin and body for 14 hours.

Finally, dawn arrived and the tide crashed in. The young orca sensed freedom. She thrashed. She strained. Volunteers pushed. Then...heave-ho, she was free! Off she swam to rejoin her family, now with a name—Miracle.

Orcas like Miracle are known as survivors, but all orcas need human help to keep their habitat—the oceans and seas—free from chemicals, noise pollution, trash, and oil spills. If we do our part, perhaps these magnificent marine mammals will survive not just for a few years but for decades to come.

▶ Miracle went on to have a calf named Magic (shown here).

Orca Family Tree

Orcas are toothed whales. Toothed whales include porpoises, whales with teeth, and dolphins. There are two types of dolphins, oceanic dolphins and river dolphins. An orca is an oceanic dolphin. This diagram shows how orcas are related to other toothed whales. The closer two animals are on the tree, the more similar they are.

Narwhals
have a long, pointy spiraled tusk that is really an enlarged tooth

Belugas
are born gray but become completely white when mature

Sperm Whales
have the largest brain of any known living animal

Porpoises
smallest of the toothed whales

Ancestor of all Toothed Whales

Note: Animal photos are not to scale.

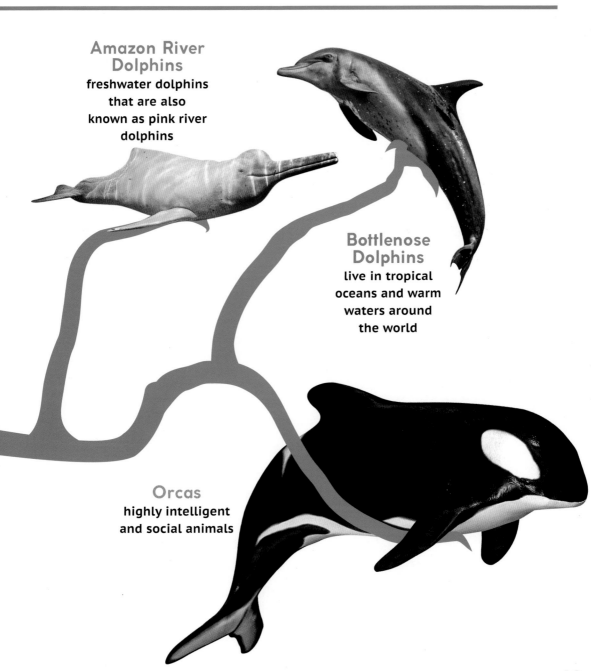

Amazon River Dolphins
freshwater dolphins that are also known as pink river dolphins

Bottlenose Dolphins
live in tropical oceans and warm waters around the world

Orcas
highly intelligent and social animals

43

Words to Know

B .... **blubber** *(BLUHB-ur)* the layer of fat under the skin of a whale, seal, or other large marine animal

C .... **carnivores** *(KAHR-nuh-vorz)* animals that eat meat

E .... **echolocation** *(EK-oh-loh-KAY-shuhn)* a way of locating distant or invisible objects using sound waves reflected back to the sender from the objects

ecotypes *(EE-koh-tipes)* distinct forms within species that are especially suited to particular environments

emits *(i-MITS)* produces or sends out something such as heat, light, signals, or sound

endangered *(en-DAYN-juhrd)* a plant or animal that is in danger of becoming extinct, usually because of human activity

F .... **fossils** *(FAH-suhls)* bones, shells, or other traces of an animal or plant from millions of years ago, preserved as rock

G .... **gestation** *(jeh-STAY-shuhn)* the period of time a baby grows and develops in its mother's body

H .... **habitat** *(HAB-i-tat)* the place where an animal or plant is usually found

hydrated *(HI-dray-ted)* supplied with sufficient amounts of fluid or moisture

I .... **ice floe** *(ISE FLOH)* a flat free mass of floating sea ice

interlocking *(in-tur-LOK-ing)* locked together

J .... **juveniles** *(JOO-vuh-nylz)* individuals in the life stage between infancy and adulthood

M .... **mammals** *(MAM-uhlz)* warm-blooded animals that have hair or fur and usually give birth to live babies; female mammals produce milk to feed their young

mate *(MATE)* to join together for breeding

matriarchal *(MAY-tree-arc-uhl)* having a female as leader of a family, group, or state

migrate *(MYE-grate)* to move to another area or climate at a particular time of year

N .... **navigate** *(NAV-i-gate)* to find where you are and where you need to go

nurse *(NURS)* to feed a baby milk from a breast

P .... **population** *(pahp-yuh-LAY-shuhn)* all members of a species living in a certain place

predators *(PRED-uh-tuhrs)* animals that live by hunting other animals for food

prey *(PRAY)* an animal that is hunted by another animal for food

S .... **species** *(SPEE-sheez)* one of the groups into which animals and plants are divided; members of the same species can mate and have offspring

stealth *(STELTH)* silence, secrecy, and caution

stunned *(STUHND)* shocked, dazed, or knocked out

V .... **vocalizations** *(VOH-kuh-li-zah-shunz)* sounds made to communicate

Find Out More

BOOKS

- Klepeis, Alicia Z. *Orcas on the Hunt* (Searchlight Books). Minneapolis, MN: Lerner Publishing Group, 2018.
- Peterson, Brenda. *Wild Orca: The Oldest, Wisest Whale in the World*. New York: Henry Holt and Co., 2018.
- Valice, Kim Perez. *The Orca Scientists* (Scientists in the Field). Boston: Houghton Mifflin Harcourt, 2018.

WEB PAGES

- kids.nationalgeographic.com/animals/orca

  This National Geographic site offers great information, cool photos, and even a video of an orca giving itself a back rub.

- www.killer-whale.org

  Visit this site to learn about orcas, their interactions with humans, and conserving their habitat.

- killerwhaletales.org

  This online education program shares field-based science regarding conservation efforts for the Southern Resident orcas.

Facts for Now

Visit this Scholastic Web site for more information on orcas: **www.factsfornow.scholastic.com** Enter the keyword Orcas

Index

Index *(continued)*

About the Author

Dionna L. Mann is a freelance journalist, an independent researcher, and a children's book writer. She loves to marvel at the amazing design found in nature—design that allows orcas to breach and seed pods to soar. Find her online at dionnalmann.com.

For their kind assistance, the author wishes to thank Giovanni Bianucci, Ph.D., Associate Professor in Paleontology, Department of Earth Sciences, University of Pisa, Italy; Ken Balcomb, Founder and Senior Scientist, Center for Whale Research, Friday Harbor, WA, US; Philip D. Gingerich, Ph.D., Curator Emeritus, Museum of Paleontology, University of Michigan, Ann Arbor, MI; and Dawn P. Noren, Ph.D. Research Fishery Biologist, NOAA NMFS Northwest Fisheries Science Center, Seattle, WA.